"In her third pub that inspire us and lift our hearts, Mary O'Connor combines her artistic eye and her poet's soul to create quiet moments for the reader. Moments punctuated by observation and insight, surprise and joy. Moments captured in stunning photographs, original watercolors, and whispers of haiku. Moments that lift the veil of passing shadows and invite us to gratefully witness the blessings of the world around us."

—JEN PAYNE, AUTHOR, *LOOK UP! MUSINGS ON THE NATURE OF MINDFULNESS*

"Mary O'Connor is a collector of calm. She naturally is drawn to it, and it to her. And when we are lucky enough to see them come together and dance—as on these pages—we smile! Our spirits are lifted and our hearts gladdened by her peaceful pirouette with words and images."

—PHIL DOUGLASS, REGIONAL OUTREACH MANAGER (RET.), UTAH DIVISION OF WILDLIFE RESOURCES

"Turning the pages of this book is like opening the windows after a hot, muggy day to find that the weather has shifted. Its haikus and accompanying photos and paintings are a mind-clearing breath of fresh air!"

—KAREN L. RANCOURT, PH.D., AUTHOR, *IT'S ALL ABOUT RELATIONSHIPS*

PASSING SHADOWS

PASSING SHADOWS
Images and Words of Inspiration

Mary O'Connor

STATION
SQUARE
≡ **MEDIA** ≡

Acknowledgements

WITH THANKS...
    To Jan Logozzo, for her friendship and her insightful photographer's eye that helped build the lifeisfullofsweetspots.com blog and this book

To Steve Plummer, for his artistic sense and design ability to turn words and images into a book that positively sings

To Janet Spencer King, for prompting the publication of this book and for guiding me through its production process

To Jen Payne, fellow writer, designer and friend, for her constant spark of creative inspiration

To all my many friends and followers of the lifeisfullofsweetspots.com blog, for their encouraging comments and good wishes

Dedication

For all who hope each day to find even a tiny bit of calming quiet and who discover in the ordinary things around them a glint of joy, a release of soothing peace

Introduction

FINDING A MEASURE of quietude is what this book is all about. It is a book of unadorned words and pictures, joined together to inspire fresh thoughts, to lift hearts or simply to bring a smile.

Science tells us that each year we travel 584 million miles around the sun. Perched on an orbiting reservoir of life called earth, we move in a grand circle through space, spinning through night and day, solar outbursts, cosmic rays.

Here, storms and shadows of social, political, environmental and physical pressures inevitably come our way. They affect our well-being and our moods, leaving us looking for a bit of celestial calming peace, even just a tiny ray of sunshine.

Photographic as well as painted images on the following pages offer meditative stopping points, reasons to pause and to think of the subject's lure. Enjoy them, rest for a minute, find what caught the camera's eye and mind's attention. Look beyond the surface and see in each a hint of inspiration, thoughts to help us get beyond the stumbling blocks of life.

Accompanying each visual image is a brief reflection expressed in the ancient Japanese poetic *haiku* format. Haikus use the barest minimum of words, structured in three lines of five-seven-five syllables, to depict a single moment in time through colorful mental imagery and natural world reference. Hallmark of a haiku is its delivery, in just one breath, of an unexpected sense of illumination.

The world on which we ride is rapidly spinning, revolving at roughly 1,000 miles per hour measured at the equator. As the world spins, and we with it, it is good to pause periodically as the ancient poet masters did and reflect on the material blessings that surround us daily.

Examine such musings and let them lead to a time of quiet, a chance to think and to breathe. Let them open our minds and relax in those unexpected feelings of "aah!"

As the title haiku, "Passing Shadows," and its accompanying photo remind us,

moments of time pass
leaving shadows in their wake
cleared away by sun

Petition

consider the trees
lifting their limbs to the sky
pageant of prayer

Winter Blues

soft dawn reflections
add veneer of warmth to time
temper winter blues

Great Lengths

stretching limbs and mind
reaching for full potential
attainable goal

Renewal

discarding darkness
trading winter's gloom for light
spring blossoms renew

Watching

keeping eyes open
watching all manner of things
life reveals wonder

Shifting Winds

waiting at corner
shifting winds change outing plans
adjust sails for new

Just Wishing

wishing is easy

daydreams bring hope within reach

attainment harder

Awakening

tiniest flowers
enfold comatose earth in joy
harbingers of spring

Gentleness

traits of tenderness
remaining still and caring
strengthen a soft heart

Feast

tasty repast draws
even simple table scraps
buoy hungry soul

Facing Forward

steps moving forward
bring future into focus
leave past in shadow

Low Tide

outgoing tides leave
rocky bottom uncovered
change is history

Rescued

adopted buddy
offers love and gratitude
rescue equals peace

Appreciation

virus met with care

hope and love seen in blue skies

flyover of thanks

Birth

life gives birth to spring
little trace of winter stress
just stretch marks of light

Force of Nature

joined at the hip
providing strength in numbers
in this together

Patience

waiting to blossom
color in all its fullness
hidden at moment

Best Buy

delightful condo
upper-level balconies
yards of trees and sky

Imitation

modeling oneself
after admired others
mimicry at best

Reaching Out

upset by chaos
empty arms wanting to help
holding out for hope

Promise

overcoming angst
unassailable hope wins
trust in country strong

Survival

left to grow alone
away from outside support
inner strength prevails

Worried

concern weighs heavy
looking for less troubled path
fly above it all

Straight Line

not always easy
switching places delicate art
manners required

Patterns

streaking across light
shadows draw contours and lines
cast patterns of life

Social Distance

neighbors and old friends
practice rules of safe distance
keep open air between

Unity

coming together

compass set on common cause

leave discord behind

Stress

storm's unfiltered force
channels stress into tailspin
enter quietness

Outdone

beauty wannabe
costumed in trendy fashion
outdone by nature

Solidarity

tiny blossoms stand
in unity with others
harmony proclaimed

Nothingness

looking at nothing
staring into bare stillness
clearing space in mind

True Beauty

grooming to attract
outward appearance invites
inner beauty binds

Closed Mind

face locked up tight
expression of narrow mind
must open to grow

Tapestry

one stem at a time
tapestry of life is built
designed for blossoms

Hard Labor

hard working bee toils
outdoor office eases stress
collects sweet payoff

Stretch

reaching up and up
beyond the top of the sky
opens unseen doors

Restorative

graced with beauty
nature's creation conveys
restorative awe

Satisfaction

meadow grass samplings
fulfill bodily cravings
simple contentment

Glory

golden light sets stage
blossoms offer breath of life
moments of peace born

Blessings

seasonal delights
stored in tiny pockets
ready for winter

Rebirth

spreading glow around
sun sinks into waiting arms
rebirth tomorrow

Purple

iconic union
power of red, peace of blue
royalty, mourning

At Rest

veiled in soft mist
haven of desired wonders
seduction at rest

Breathe

soft whisper of leaves
sounds of silence nature's song
calming naptime tune

Depreciated

spit and polish gone
newfangled life edges in
old charm forgotten

Wasted

nothing achieved
time spent just sitting around
use it or lose it

Diversities

difference divides
when the mind stops at color
likenesses unseen

Bad Humor

blinded by temper
ability to laugh gone
better to calm down

Sheltered

all looks beautiful
sheltered from divisive truth
distorted vision

Rise Up

drawn by dawning hope
leaves security behind
rises to new heights

Bold

showy purple spears
timidity on notice
riot of chutzpa

Hope

two Finch, feathers of rose,
build nest of softness and love
birth of hope and song

Solitude

weighted with worry
resting now in quieting space
silence boosts the soul

Keep Moving

sustain momentum
treading water not enough
take active measures

Departure

streamlets of water
telling signs of departure
teardrops of leaving

Puffed Up

inflated with pride
feeding on vibes of vanity
hyped up beauty

Reflections

reflection of time
mirrors depth of existence
future still unseen

Hanging Out

while just staying put
life continues around us
over and over

World Outlook

perched high on top
troubled world outlook gained
best keep feet on ground

Leftovers

the half-eaten dish
to be served tomorrow
blessed leftovers

Looking Forward

darkness edges in
gilded shadows tell what's done
sign of more to come

Alteration

ripples in water
reflections delusional
distortions of truth

Refuge

quiet seeps inward
soothes and calms beneath surface
numbing sedative

Uncertain

maybe it is safe
leaving this place of cover
to chance risky life

Mischief

just stirring things up
tempering good with trouble
laughter escapes eyes

Anxious

hiding quietly
watching something not right
better to speak up

Absorbing

learning at young age
builds future understanding
worthwhile fixation

Ingenuity

strength of conviction
fuels force of cleverness
new ways of working

Smiles

never ending smile
expresses message of love
signature of joy

152

Enthralled

wonder is trapped
in the lens of children's eyes
trusting enchantment

Empathy

reaching out in space
focusing beyond one's self
truly connecting

Passing Shadows

moments of time pass
leaving shadows in their wake
cleared away by sun

Photo by Jan Logozzo

About the Author

MARY O'CONNOR IS a writer, poet, painter and lover of nature. She is the author of "Life Is Full of Sweet Spots—An Exploration of Joy" as well as "Dreams of a Wingless Child," a collection of award-winning nature and inspirational verses. Mary often complements her writings with visual images of photography as well as paintings in watercolors and acrylics. Her watercolor paintings have been exhibited by area art associations, and her animal portraits are treasured by numerous individual pet owners.

A popular public speaker and workshop facilitator, Mary has also taught poetry writing to inmates at the Connecticut state prison for women, and has served as a docent at an American Impressionist art museum and as a volunteer in the community arena. She lives along the Connecticut shoreline where she conceives much of her work.

About Warrior Expeditions

Warrior Expeditions helps veterans transition from their wartime experiences through therapeutic outdoor expeditions. Since its founding in 2013 as a nonprofit 501(c)3 organization, Warrior Expeditions has sent returning servicemen and women on extended forays into the wild as a way of decompressing and reintegrating into society.

Outings take anywhere from three to six months and include eight trails, plus a Mississippi River kayak voyage and a cross-country bicycle trek. Warrior Expeditions provides the gear, clothing, supplies, a small monthly stipend and skills training needed to complete expeditions and for readjustment to civilian life after a combat zone. The camaraderie experienced with other veterans helps restore faith in humanity and build an important network of life-long friendships and relationships.

All proceeds from the sale of Passing Shadows will be donated to the nonprofit Warrior Expeditions organization in support of its therapeutic programs that help veterans transition from their wartime experiences through outdoor expeditions. (www.warriorexpeditions.org)

Images Credits

PHOTOS BY MARY O'CONNOR

WATERCOLOR PAINTINGS
BY MARY O'CONNOR

Made in the USA
Monee, IL
01 November 2021

80665264R00100